WITHDRAWN

D1313975

WITHDRAWN

SABER-TOOTHED CAT

by Harold T. Rober

BUMBA BOOKS™

LERNER PUBLICATIONS ◆ MINNEAPOLIS

Note to Educators:

Throughout this book, you'll find critical thinking questions. These can be used to engage young readers in thinking critically about the topic and in using the text and photos to do so.

Copyright © 2017 by Lerner Publishing Group, Inc.

All rights reserved. International copyright secured. No part of this book may be reproduced, stored in a retrieval system, or transmitted in any form or by any means—electronic, mechanical, photocopying, recording, or otherwise—without the prior written permission of Lerner Publishing Group, Inc., except for the inclusion of brief quotations in an acknowledged review.

Lerner Publications Company
A division of Lerner Publishing Group, Inc.
241 First Avenue North
Minneapolis, MN 55401 USA

For reading levels and more information, look up this title at www.lernerbooks.com.

Library of Congress Cataloging-in-Publication Data

Names: Rober, Harold T.
Title: Saber-toothed cat / by Harold T. Rober.
Description: Minneapolis : Lerner Publications, [2017] | Series: Bumba books—Dinosaurs and prehistoric beasts |
    Audience: Age 4–8. | Audience: K to grade 3. | Includes bibliographical references and index.
Identifiers: LCCN 2016018695 (print) | LCCN 2016019818 (ebook) | ISBN 9781512426458 (lb : alk. paper) |
    ISBN 9781512429152 (pb : alk. paper) | ISBN 9781512427394 (eb pdf)
Subjects: LCSH: Saber-toothed tigers—Juvenile literature.
Classification: LCC QE882.C15 R63 2017 (print) | LCC QE882.C15 (ebook) | DDC 569/.75—dc23

LC record available at https://lccn.loc.gov/2016018695

Manufactured in the United States of America
1 – VP – 12/31/16

Expand learning beyond the printed book. Download free, complementary educational resources for this book from our website, www.lerneresource.com.

Table of Contents

Saber-Toothed Cat Roared

Saber-toothed cat was a mammal.

It lived thousands of years ago.

It is extinct.

This cat had sharp teeth.

Two of its teeth were very long.

What might an animal do with such long teeth?

Saber-toothed cat

ate meat.

This cat hid in bushes.

It jumped out when prey

was near.

Saber-toothed cat opened its

mouth wide.

It used its long teeth to kill prey.

Saber-toothed cat had

sharp claws.

These claws helped it eat and fight.

How do you think sharp claws helped saber-toothed cat eat and fight?

Saber-toothed cat
was big and heavy.

It was as tall as a lion.

It weighed as much as
two lions.

Saber-toothed cat lived in areas
with tall grass.
It also lived in areas with trees
and bushes.

Saber-toothed cats lived
in groups called packs.
Cats in a pack worked
together to catch prey.

Saber-toothed cat roared.

It showed its long teeth.

Why do you think this cat roared?

Parts of a Saber-Toothed Cat

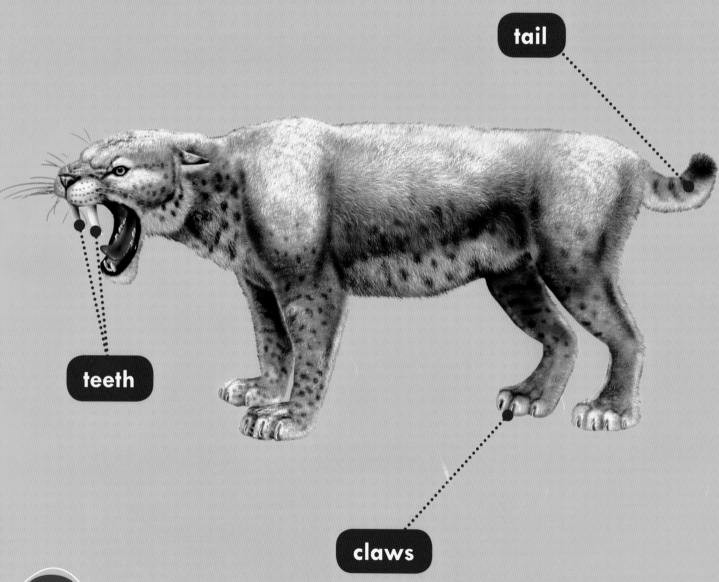

tail

teeth

claws

Picture Glossary

extinct

no longer alive

mammal

a warm-blooded animal with fur

packs

groups of similar animals

prey

an animal that is hunted by another animal

23

Index

Read More

Carr, Aaron. *Saber-Toothed Cat*. New York: AV2 by Weigl, 2015.

Rober, Harold T. *Woolly Mammoth*. Minneapolis: Lerner Publications, 2017.

Zabludoff, Marc. *Saber-Toothed Cat*. New York: Marshall Cavendish Benchmark, 2011.

Photo Credits

The images in this book are used with the permission of: © Corey A. Ford/Dreamstime.com, pp. 5, 23 (top right); © Sasha Samardzija/Shutterstock.com, pp. 6, 23 (top left); © Catmando/Shutterstock.com, pp. 8–9, 14–15, 17, 18–19, 23 (bottom left), 23 (bottom right); © Valentyna Chukhlyebova/Shutterstock.com, pp. 10, 13; © Ozja/Shutterstock.com, pp. 21, 22.

Front Cover: © tsuneomp/Shutterstock.com.